MW01612658

GOD IS AMONG YOU

THE PROPHECIES OF NAHUM, HABAKKUK, ZEPHANIAH, AND HAGGAI

HE READS TRUTH

HE READS TRUTH

EDITORIAL

EDITORS-IN-CHIEF
Raechel Myers & Amanda Bible Williams

CONTENT DIRECTOR
Russ Ramsey, MDiv., ThM.

MANAGING EDITOR
Jessica Lamb

EDITORS
Kara Gause
Matt Erickson

EDITORIAL ASSISTANT
Ellen Taylor

CREATIVE

CREATIVE DIRECTOR
Ryan Myers

ART DIRECTOR
Amanda Barnhart

DESIGNER
Kelsea Allen

SUPPORTING DESIGNER
Emily Knapp

PRODUCTION DESIGNER
Julie Allen

All photography used by permission.

@hereadstruth

hereadstruth.com

SUBSCRIPTION INQUIRIES
orders@hereadstruth.com

COLOPHON

This book was printed offset in Nashville, Tennessee, on 60# Lynx Opaque Text under the direction of He Reads Truth. The cover is 100# matte with a soft touch aqueous coating.

COPYRIGHT

ISBN 978-1-946282-84-2

Though the dates in this book have been carefully researched, scholars disagree on the dating of many biblical events.

"God is great, God is good, let us thank Him for our food."

Many of us learned this simple prayer in childhood. Though basic, the first line communicates an essential truth about our God.

God is great. He is powerful, sovereign, and holy. He created the world and everything in it (Jr 32:27; Ac 17:24). He is just (Rm 12:19). He alone can rescue us from suffering, despair, and the deeply felt ramifications of sin (Is 43:11).

God is good. He is close to His people (Dt 4:7). He is compassionate and gracious (Ps 86:15). He is abounding in mercy and kindness. He is faithful even when we are not (Ex 34:6–7; 2Tm 2:13). His goodness and love are on display through the work of Jesus, inviting us to know Him and belong to Him even in our rebellion and sin (Rm 5:8).

God is always fully Himself. In the Minor Prophets, we read about God's character: He is present. He is active. He mourns, hurts, and acts in righteous anger. He comforts, rebukes, and restores. While the Minor Prophets show us the devastating consequences of sin, they also paint a picture of a God who is fully just, fully loving, and fully good in His response to wayward hearts and brokenness.

This book presents four Minor Prophets in one cohesive study: Nahum, Habakkuk, Zephaniah, and Haggai. These books of the Bible also cover a large swath of Israel's history, which you'll see in the timeline on page 44.

We pray these resources better equip you to read and understand God's Word, pointing you toward a God who is great, good, and deeply invested in His people.

Read on,

THE HE READS TRUTH TEAM

"The muted color palette is inspired by old leather goods, aged library shelves, and tattered book cloth."

Reading the Minor Prophets requires thoughtful study and perseverance. For this reason, we wanted this book to have a scholarly look. A marbled composition book texture is used throughout to give an academic feel and to encourage note-taking.

You might recognize the wayfinding tool from our last study of the Minor Prophets. It's stamped on the first page of each day's reading and quickly orients you to the book you're in as well as the order in which it falls among the others.

For this study we chose the serif font Baskerville for its classic legibility and character, and paired it with the more stoic, understated Franklin Gothic for an informative yet functional design.

The muted color palette is inspired by old leather goods, aged library shelves, and tattered book cloth—items that are built to endure the passage of time.

The book of Haggai, included in this study, reminds us that our choices matter and should draw us back to God. Even decisions as small as the typeface or color scheme can enhance our experience of studying Scripture, and that was our goal in each design choice we made.

THE HE READS TRUTH CREATIVE TEAM

HOW TO USE THIS BOOK

Each book in the He Reads Truth Legacy Series™ provides space to read and study Scripture, make notes, and record prayers. As you build your library, you will have a record of your Bible-reading journey to reference and pass down.

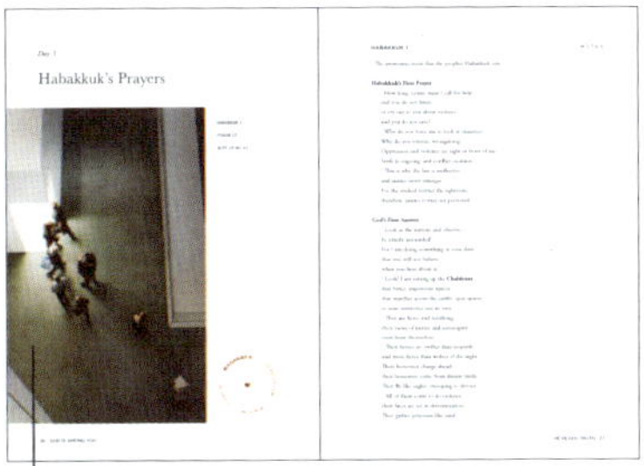

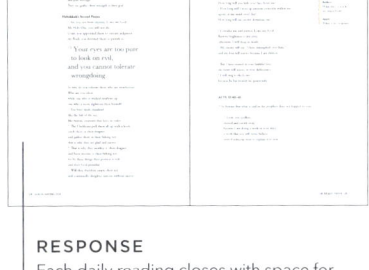

SCRIPTURE READING PLAN

Designed for a Monday start, this Legacy Book presents the books of Nahum, Habakkuk, Zephaniah, and Haggai in daily readings, plus supplemental passages for additional context.

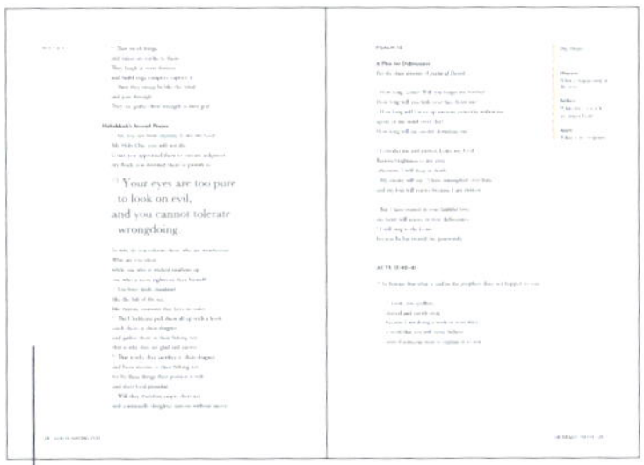

RESPONSE

Each daily reading closes with space for notes and prayers.

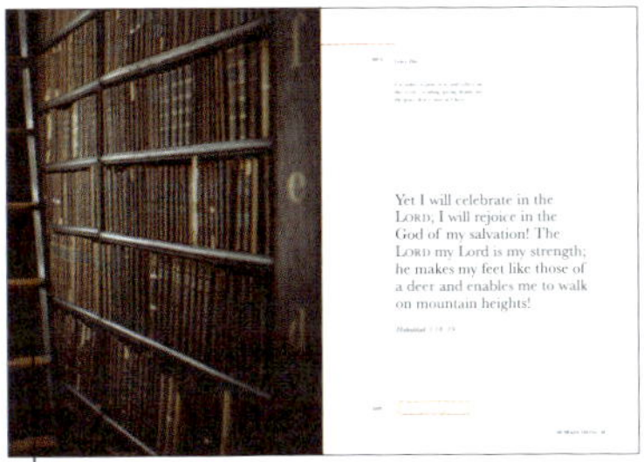

GRACE DAY

Use Saturdays to pray, rest, and reflect on what you've read.

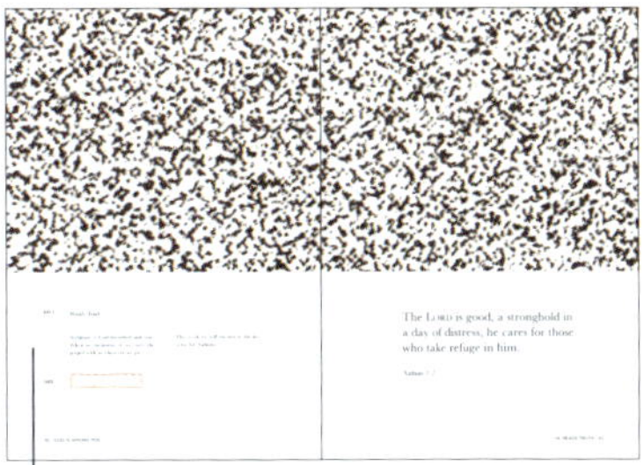

WEEKLY TRUTH

Sundays are set aside for weekly Scripture memorization.

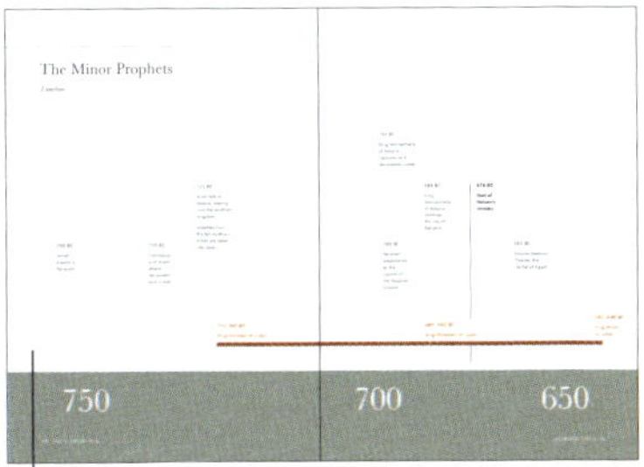

EXTRAS

This book features additional tools to help you gain a deeper understanding of the text.

For additional commentary on each day's reading, download the He Reads Truth™ app and choose the **Nahum, Habakkuk, Zephaniah, and Haggai** reading plan, or follow along at HeReadsTruth.com.

TABLE OF CONTENTS

Week 1

Nahum

Habakkuk

EXTRAS

Week 2

Zephaniah

Haggai

HOW TO READ PROPHETS AND PROPHECY

Books of prophecy make up nearly half of the Old Testament. To understand these writings, we need to first understand the role of the prophet, the nature of prophecy, and the most common forms of prophetic speech.

OLD TESTAMENT

Prophets

THEY WERE APPOINTED BY GOD.	Prophets did not appoint themselves. God pronounced harsh judgment on false prophets because they assumed authority but did not speak God's Word.
THEY WERE MESSENGERS.	Prophets in the Old Testament were people called to deliver a message from God. Their words were not their own.
THEY WERE INSIDERS.	Prophets usually were part of the people God called them to address. Their message applied to themselves as well as to their audiences.
THEY HAD AUTHORITY.	Prophets held an official position, similar to the roles of priests and kings. They had authority and were meant to be able to speak God's truth to people in power without fear of retribution.

OLD TESTAMENT

Prophecy

IT WAS SELDOM A NEW MESSAGE.	Most of the prophets did not deliver new laws. They usually called Israel to obey God's existing law.
IT WAS READ ALOUD.	Prophecies were originally delivered as messages spoken to a public audience. The prophets were heard before they were read.
IT WAS RELATIONAL.	Although the prophetic books often deal with subjects like famine, displacement, and God's judgment, the fact that they exist shows that God is in an ongoing relationship with His people.
THE DARKER IT GETS, THE BIGGER THE CROSS APPEARS.	The bleak imagery of the Old Testament prophets shows people are without hope apart from a redeemer. Christ went to the cross to atone for the darkest realities described in the prophetic books.

Types of Prophecy

THE MESSENGER'S SPEECH

1

Often beginning with "Thus says the Lord," this is the most common form of prophecy. The prophet reminds his audience that he is only the messenger and is therefore one of them.

THE LAWSUIT

2

God is the plaintiff, judge, prosecutor, and bailiff in a court case against the defendant, usually a nation. The lawsuit contains, either explicitly or implicitly, a summons, a reading of charges, evidence, and a verdict.

THE WOE

3

A cry in the face of disaster, this form of prophecy includes a call of distress, the reason for the distress, and the predicted fate of the person or group in distress.

THE PROMISE

4

Promising salvation, this kind of prophecy is comprised of a reference to the future, a promise of coming change, and the guarantee of blessing.

THE ENACTMENT

5

The prophet not only speaks God's Word, but symbolically acts it out in some way.

NAHUM · HABAKKUK · ZEPHANIAH · HAGGAI

KEY VERSE

The LORD is good, a stronghold in a day of distress; he cares for those who take refuge in him.

Nahum 1:7

ON THE TIMELINE

Nahum was written sometime between the capture and downfall of Thebes (the capital of Egypt) in 663 BC and the destruction of Nineveh in 612 BC. The northern kingdom of Israel had been overthrown by Assyria about a century earlier, and Nahum's message was meant to bring comfort to the remaining kingdom of Judah as it pronounced God's judgment on the enemies of God's people. Jonah's message to Nineveh occurred about 100 years prior to Nahum's. While God relented from sending judgment on Nineveh in Jonah's day, Nahum announced that God's judgment against this wicked nation was now certain.

A LITTLE BACKGROUND

Nahum the Elkoshite (Nah 1:1) is the only person identified by that name in the Old Testament. Like Jonah in the previous century, Nahum prophesied judgment upon Nineveh. The Ninevites in Jonah's time had repented (Jnh 3), but now that Nineveh's leaders had resumed their wicked actions, God called Nahum to reaffirm God's coming judgment. Ironically, Nahum's Hebrew name means "comfort"—comfort for Judah (Nah 1:12-15) because its cruel overlord Assyria would be punished without any comforters (Nah 3:7).

MESSAGE & PURPOSE

The main theme of the book of Nahum is the Lord's impending judgment of Nineveh (Nah 1:1, 8; 2:8-13; 3:7-19) by which He would deliver His people (Nah 1:12-15). The Lord would punish Nineveh in the same way they had mistreated their enemies. God, portrayed as a powerful but caring warrior (Nah 1:2-7), was the propelling force behind Nineveh's judgment. God's wrath is consistent with His promise to avenge the blood of His servants (Dt 32:35-36, 42-43). He was "good" (or kind) to those who took refuge in Him (Nah 1:7), while bringing destruction on His unrepentant enemies, including Nineveh (Nah 1:8).

Day 1

God's Vengeance

NAHUM 1, 2 KINGS 19:8-19

NAHUM 1

[1] The pronouncement concerning Nineveh. The book of the vision of Nahum the **Elkoshite.**

God's Vengeance

[2] The LORD is a jealous and avenging God;
the LORD takes vengeance
and is fierce in wrath.
The LORD takes vengeance against his foes;
he is furious with his enemies.

[3] The LORD is slow to anger but great in power; the LORD will never leave the guilty unpunished.

His path is in the whirlwind and storm,
and clouds are the dust beneath his feet.
[4] He rebukes the sea and dries it up,
and he makes all the rivers run dry.
Bashan and **Carmel** wither;
even the flower of **Lebanon** withers.
[5] The mountains quake before him,
and the hills melt;
the earth trembles at his presence—
the world and all who live in it.

Glossary Terms

-

Key people and places in **bold** are featured in the glossary beginning on page 80.

[6] Who can withstand his indignation?
Who can endure his burning anger?
His wrath is poured out like fire;
even rocks are shattered before him.

Destruction of Nineveh

[7] The LORD is good,
a stronghold in a day of distress;
he cares for those who take refuge in him.
[8] But he will completely destroy **Nineveh**
with an overwhelming flood,
and he will chase his enemies into darkness.

[9] Whatever you plot against the LORD,
he will bring it to complete destruction;
oppression will not rise up a second time.
[10] For they will be consumed
like entangled thorns,
like the drink of a drunkard
and like straw that is fully dry.
[11] One has gone out from you,
who plots evil against the LORD,
and is a wicked counselor.

Promise of Judah's Deliverance

[12] This is what the LORD says:

Though they are strong and numerous,
they will still be mowed down,
and he will pass away.

NOTES

Though I have punished you,
I will punish you no longer.
13 For I will now break off his yoke from you
and tear off your shackles.

The Assyrian King's Demise

14 The LORD has issued an order concerning you:

There will be no offspring
to carry on your name.
I will eliminate the carved idol and cast image
from the house of your gods;
I will prepare your grave,
for you are contemptible.

15 Look to the mountains—
the feet of the herald,
who proclaims peace.
Celebrate your festivals, **Judah**;
fulfill your vows.
For the wicked one will never again
march through you;
he will be entirely wiped out.

2 KINGS 19:8–19

Sennacherib's Departing Threat

8 When the royal spokesman heard that the king of **Assyria** had pulled
out of **Lachish**, he left and found him fighting against Libnah. 9 The
king had heard concerning King Tirhakah of **Cush**, "Look, he has set out
to fight against you." So he again sent messengers to **Hezekiah**, saying,
10 "Say this to King Hezekiah of Judah: 'Don't let your God, on whom
you rely, deceive you by promising that **Jerusalem** will not be handed
over to the king of Assyria. 11 Look, you have heard what the kings of
Assyria have done to all the countries: They completely destroyed them.
Will you be rescued? 12 Did the gods of the nations that my predecessors
destroyed rescue them—nations such as Gozan, Haran, Rezeph, and the

Edenites in Telassar? [13] Where is the king of Hamath, the king of Arpad, the king of the city of Sepharvaim, Hena, or Ivvah?'"

Hezekiah's Prayer

[14] Hezekiah took the letter from the messengers' hands, read it, then went up to the LORD's temple, and spread it out before the LORD. [15] Then Hezekiah prayed before the LORD:

> LORD God of Israel, enthroned between the cherubim, you are God—you alone—of all the kingdoms of the earth. You made the heavens and the earth. [16] Listen closely, LORD, and hear; open your eyes, LORD, and see. Hear the words that **Sennacherib** has sent to mock the living God. [17] LORD, it is true that the kings of Assyria have devastated the nations and their lands. [18] They have thrown their gods into the fire, for they were not gods but made by human hands—wood and stone. So they have destroyed them. [19] Now, LORD our God, please save us from his power so that all the kingdoms of the earth may know that you, LORD, are God—you alone.

Dig Deeper

-

Observe
What is happening in the text?

Reflect
What does it teach me about God?

Apply
What is my response?

Day 2

Attack Against Nineveh

NAHUM 2-3, 2 CHRONICLES 32:9-23

NAHUM 2

Attack Against Nineveh

1 One who scatters is coming up against you.
Man the fortifications!
Watch the road!
Brace yourself!
Summon all your strength!

2 For the LORD will restore the majesty of Jacob,
yes, the majesty of **Israel**,
though ravagers have ravaged them
and ruined their vine branches.

3 The shields of his warriors are dyed red;
the valiant men are dressed in scarlet.
The fittings of the chariot flash like fire
on the day of its battle preparations,
and the spears are brandished.
4 The chariots dash madly through the streets;
they rush around in the plazas.
They look like torches;
they dart back and forth like lightning.
5 He gives orders to his officers;
they stumble as they advance.
They race to its wall;
the protective shield is set in place.
6 The river gates are opened,
and the palace erodes away.

7 Beauty is stripped;
she is carried away;
her ladies-in-waiting moan
like the sound of doves
and beat their breasts.
8 Nineveh has been like a pool of water
from her first days,
but they are fleeing.
"Stop! Stop!" they cry,
but no one turns back.
9 "Plunder the silver! Plunder the gold!"
There is no end to the treasure,
an abundance of every precious thing.
10 Desolation, decimation, devastation!
Hearts melt,
knees tremble,
insides churn,
every face grows pale!

11 Where is the lions' lair,
or the feeding ground of the young lions,
where the lion and lioness prowled,
and the lion's cub,
with nothing to frighten them away?
12 The lion mauled whatever its cubs needed
and strangled prey for its lionesses.
It filled up its dens with the kill,
and its lairs with mauled prey.
13 Beware, I am against you.
This is the declaration of the **Lord of Armies**.

NOTES

I will make your chariots go up in smoke,
and the sword will devour your young lions.
I will cut off your prey from the earth,
and the sound of your messengers
will never be heard again.

NAHUM 3

Nineveh's Downfall

1 Woe to the city of blood,
totally deceitful,
full of plunder,
never without prey.
2 The crack of the whip
and rumble of the wheel,
galloping horse
and jolting chariot!
3 Charging horseman,
flashing sword,
shining spear;
heaps of slain,
mounds of corpses,
dead bodies without end—
they stumble over their dead.
4 Because of the continual prostitution of the prostitute,
the attractive mistress of sorcery,
who treats nations and clans like merchandise
by her prostitution and sorcery,
5 I am against you.
This is the declaration of the LORD of Armies.
I will lift your skirts over your face
and display your nakedness to nations,
your shame to kingdoms.
6 I will throw filth on you
and treat you with contempt;
I will make a spectacle of you.
7 Then all who see you will recoil from you, saying,
"Nineveh is devastated;

who will show sympathy to her?"
Where can I find anyone to comfort you?

8 Are you better than **Thebes**
that sat along the **Nile**
with water surrounding her,
whose rampart was the sea,
the river her wall?
9 Cush and **Egypt** were her endless source of strength;
Put and **Libya** were among her allies.
10 Yet she became an exile;
she went into captivity.
Her children were also dashed to pieces
at the head of every street.
They cast lots for her dignitaries,
and all her nobles were bound in chains.
11 You also will become drunk;
you will hide.
You also will seek refuge from the enemy.

12 All your fortresses are fig trees
with figs that ripened first;
when shaken, they fall—
right into the mouth of the eater!

13 Look, your troops are like women among you;
your land's city gates
are wide open to your enemies.
Fire will devour the bars of your gates.

14 Draw water for the siege;
strengthen your fortresses.
Step into the clay and tread the mortar;
take hold of the brick-mold!
15 The fire will devour you there;
the sword will cut you down.
It will devour you like the young locust.
Multiply yourselves like the young locust;
multiply like the swarming locust!

NOTES

NOTES

[16] You have made your merchants
more numerous than the stars of the sky.
The young locust strips the land
and flies away.
[17] Your court officials are like the swarming locust,
and your scribes like clouds of locusts,
which settle on the walls on a cold day;
when the sun rises, they take off,
and no one knows where they are.

[18] **King of Assyria**, your shepherds slumber;
your officers sleep.
Your people are scattered across the mountains
with no one to gather them together.
[19] There is no remedy for your injury;
your wound is severe.

All who hear the news about you will clap their hands because of you,

for who has not experienced
your constant cruelty?

2 CHRONICLES 32:9–23

Sennacherib's Servant's Speech

[9] After this, while King Sennacherib of Assyria with all his armed forces
besieged Lachish, he sent his servants to Jerusalem against King Hezekiah
of Judah and against all those of Judah who were in Jerusalem, saying,
[10] "This is what King Sennacherib of Assyria says: 'What are you relying
on that you remain in Jerusalem under siege? [11] Isn't Hezekiah misleading
you to give you over to death by famine and thirst when he says, "The
Lord our God will keep us from the grasp of the king of Assyria"?
[12] Didn't Hezekiah himself remove his high places and his altars and say
to Judah and Jerusalem, "You must worship before one altar, and you
must burn incense on it"?

[13] "'Don't you know what I and my fathers have done to all the peoples
of the lands? Have any of the national gods of the lands been able to
rescue their land from my power? [14] Who among all the gods of these
nations that my predecessors completely destroyed was able to rescue his
people from my power, that your God should be able to deliver you from
my power? [15] So now, don't let Hezekiah deceive you, and don't let him
mislead you like this. Don't believe him, for no god of any nation or
kingdom has been able to rescue his people from my power or the power
of my fathers. How much less will your God rescue you from my power!'"

[16] His servants said more against the LORD God and against his servant
Hezekiah. [17] He also wrote letters to mock the LORD, the God of Israel,
saying against him:

> Just like the national gods of the lands that did not rescue their people from my power, so Hezekiah's God will not rescue his people from my power.

[18] Then they called out loudly in Hebrew to the people of Jerusalem, who
were on the wall, to frighten and discourage them in order that he might
capture the city. [19] They spoke against the God of Jerusalem like they had
spoken against the gods of the peoples of the earth, which were made by
human hands.

Deliverance from Sennacherib

[20] King Hezekiah and the prophet Isaiah son of Amoz prayed about this
and cried out to heaven, [21] and the LORD sent an angel who annihilated
every valiant warrior, leader, and commander in the camp of the king of
Assyria. So the king of Assyria returned in disgrace to his land. He went
to the temple of his god, and there some of his own children struck him
down with the sword.

[22] So the LORD saved Hezekiah and the inhabitants of Jerusalem from the
power of King Sennacherib of Assyria and from the power of all others.
He gave them rest on every side. [23] Many were bringing an offering to the
LORD to Jerusalem and valuable gifts to King Hezekiah of Judah, and he
was exalted in the eyes of all the nations after that.

Dig Deeper

-

Observe
What is happening in the text?

Reflect
What does it teach me about God?

Apply
What is my response?

GIVE THANKS FOR THE BOOK OF

Nahum

The book of Nahum depicts a powerful and just God who maintains His absolute moral standards and offers hope to those who are despised and downtrodden. Nahum teaches us to trust in God. Even when our situation seems hopeless, Nahum's message reminds us that God will stand with those who belong to Him.

HABAKKUK · ZEPHANIAH · HAGGAI · NAHUM

KEY VERSE

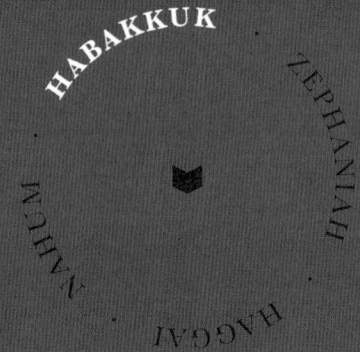

Yet I will celebrate in the LORD; I will rejoice in the God of my salvation! The LORD my Lord is my strength; he makes my feet like those of a deer and enables me to walk on mountain heights!

Habakkuk 3:18-19

ON THE TIMELINE

Habakkuk likely wrote his prophecy after the death of King Josiah of Judah in 609 BC but before the devastations of Judah in 597 BC and 586 BC. This dates the prophecy to the reign of Jehoiakim (around 609–599 BC), probably in the period of Egyptian domination before Babylon invaded Judah (609–605 BC).

A LITTLE BACKGROUND

Rather than speaking to the people on God's behalf, Habakkuk spoke to God on behalf of the people. The entire small book of Habakkuk is a conversation between Habakkuk and the Lord. This conversation predicts the Babylonian devastation of Judah (Hab 1:5–11), a prophecy fulfilled when Nebuchadnezzar invaded Jerusalem and destroyed the temple in 586 BC. Habakkuk also predicts Babylon's own day of reckoning (Hab 2:6–20), which occurred when Cyrus of Persia conquered Babylon in 539 BC.

MESSAGE & PURPOSE

Habakkuk deals with the human problem of understanding God's ways: How can God allow injustice to prevail (Hab 1:3)? Why does God use the more wicked Babylonians to punish the less wicked Judeans (Hab 1:13)? How long will God allow evildoers to dominate the world (Hab 1:17)? Rather than giving clear answers to these questions Habakkuk raised, God instructed the godly to have faith (Hab 2:4).

Habakkuk also demonstrates the greatness of God: He is eternally alive (Hab 1:12), He can raise up nations to accomplish His purposes (Hab 1:6), and He shakes the world through pestilence and war (Hab 3:2–15). Though God may use the wicked acts of men for His good purposes and allow evil to prevail for a time, ultimately the wicked will pay for their crimes (Hab 2:6–14), and God will come to save His people and crush the wicked (Hab 3:13–15).

Day 3

Habakkuk's Prayers

HABAKKUK 1

PSALM 13

ACTS 13:40–41

1 The pronouncement that the prophet Habakkuk saw.

Habakkuk's First Prayer

2 How long, LORD, must I call for help
and you do not listen
or cry out to you about violence
and you do not save?
3 Why do you force me to look at injustice?
Why do you tolerate wrongdoing?
Oppression and violence are right in front of me.
Strife is ongoing, and conflict escalates.
4 This is why the law is ineffective
and justice never emerges.
For the wicked restrict the righteous;
therefore, justice comes out perverted.

God's First Answer

5 Look at the nations and observe—
be utterly astounded!
For I am doing something in your days
that you will not believe
when you hear about it.
6 Look! I am raising up the **Chaldeans**,
that bitter, impetuous nation
that marches across the earth's open spaces
to seize territories not its own.
7 They are fierce and terrifying;
their views of justice and sovereignty
stem from themselves.
8 Their horses are swifter than leopards
and more fierce than wolves of the night.
Their horsemen charge ahead;
their horsemen come from distant lands.
They fly like eagles, swooping to devour.
9 All of them come to do violence;
their faces are set in determination.
They gather prisoners like sand.

NOTES

[10] They mock kings,
and rulers are a joke to them.
They laugh at every fortress
and build siege ramps to capture it.
[11] Then they sweep by like the wind
and pass through.
They are guilty; their strength is their god.

Habakkuk's Second Prayer

[12] Are you not from eternity, LORD my God?
My Holy One, you will not die.
LORD, you appointed them to execute judgment;
my Rock, you destined them to punish us.

[13] Your eyes are too pure to look on evil, and you cannot tolerate wrongdoing.

So why do you tolerate those who are treacherous?
Why are you silent
while one who is wicked swallows up
one who is more righteous than himself?
[14] You have made mankind
like the fish of the sea,
like marine creatures that have no ruler.
[15] The Chaldeans pull them all up with a hook,
catch them in their dragnet,
and gather them in their fishing net;
that is why they are glad and rejoice.
[16] That is why they sacrifice to their dragnet
and burn incense to their fishing net,
for by these things their portion is rich
and their food plentiful.
[17] Will they therefore empty their net
and continually slaughter nations without mercy?

PSALM 13

A Plea for Deliverance

For the choir director. A psalm of David.

1 How long, LORD? Will you forget me forever?
How long will you hide your face from me?
2 How long will I store up anxious concerns within me,
agony in my mind every day?
How long will my enemy dominate me?

3 Consider me and answer, LORD my God.
Restore brightness to my eyes;
otherwise, I will sleep in death.
4 My enemy will say, "I have triumphed over him,"
and my foes will rejoice because I am shaken.

5 But I have trusted in your faithful love;
my heart will rejoice in your deliverance.
6 I will sing to the LORD
because he has treated me generously.

ACTS 13:40–41

40 So beware that what is said in the prophets does not happen to you:

> 41 Look, you scoffers,
> marvel and vanish away,
> because I am doing a work in your days,
> a work that you will never believe,
> even if someone were to explain it to you.

Dig Deeper

-

Observe
What is happening in the text?

Reflect
What does it teach me about God?

Apply
What is my response?

Day 4

The Five Woe Oracles

HABAKKUK 2

PROVERBS 29:18

HEBREWS 10:32-39

HABAKKUK · ZEPHANIAH · HAGGAI · NAHUM

Habakkuk Waits for God's Response

1 I will stand at my guard post
and station myself on the lookout tower.
I will watch to see what he will say to me
and what I should reply about my complaint.

God's Second Answer

2 The LORD answered me:

Write down this vision;
clearly inscribe it on tablets
so one may easily read it.
3 For the vision is yet for the appointed time;
it testifies about the end and will not lie.
Though it delays, wait for it,
since it will certainly come and not be late.
4 Look, his ego is inflated;
he is without integrity.
But the righteous one will live by his faith.
5 Moreover, wine betrays;
an arrogant man is never at rest.
He enlarges his appetite like **Sheol**,
and like Death he is never satisfied.
He gathers all the nations to himself;
he collects all the peoples for himself.

The Five Woe Oracles

6 Won't all of these take up a taunt against him,
with mockery and riddles about him?
They will say:
Woe to him who amasses what is not his—
how much longer?—
and loads himself with goods taken in pledge.
7 Won't your creditors suddenly arise,
and those who disturb you wake up?
Then you will become spoil for them.
8 Since you have plundered many nations,
all the peoples who remain will plunder you—

NOTES

because of human bloodshed
and violence against lands, cities,
and all who live in them.

9 Woe to him who dishonestly makes
wealth for his house
to place his nest on high,
to escape the grasp of disaster!
10 You have planned shame for your house
by wiping out many peoples
and sinning against your own self.
11 For the stones will cry out from the wall,
and the rafters will answer them
from the woodwork.

12 Woe to him who builds a city with bloodshed
and founds a town with injustice!
13 Is it not from the LORD of Armies
that the peoples labor only to fuel the fire
and countries exhaust themselves for nothing?
14 For the earth will be filled
with the knowledge of the LORD's glory,
as the water covers the sea.

15 Woe to him who gives his neighbors drink,
pouring out your wrath
and even making them drunk,
in order to look at their nakedness!
16 You will be filled with disgrace instead of glory.
You also—drink,
and expose your uncircumcision!
The cup in the LORD's right hand
will come around to you,
and utter disgrace will cover your glory.
17 For your violence against Lebanon
will overwhelm you;
the destruction of animals will terrify you
because of your human bloodshed and violence
against lands, cities, and all who live in them.

18 What use is a carved idol
after its craftsman carves it?
It is only a cast image, a teacher of lies.
For the one who crafts its shape trusts in it
and makes idols that cannot speak.
19 Woe to him who says to wood: Wake up!
or to mute stone: Come alive!
Can it teach?
Look! It may be plated with gold and silver,
yet there is no breath in it at all.

20 But the LORD is in his holy temple;
let the whole earth
be silent in his presence.

Dig Deeper

-

Observe
What is happening in the text?

Reflect
What does it teach me about God?

Apply
What is my response?

PROVERBS 29:18

Without revelation people run wild,
but one who follows divine instruction will be happy.

HEBREWS 10:32–39

32 Remember the earlier days when, after you had been enlightened,
you endured a hard struggle with sufferings. 33 Sometimes you were
publicly exposed to taunts and afflictions, and at other times you were
companions of those who were treated that way. 34 For you sympathized
with the prisoners and accepted with joy the confiscation of your
possessions, because you know that you yourselves have a better and
enduring possession. 35 So don't throw away your confidence, which has
a great reward. 36 For you need endurance, so that after you have done
God's will, you may receive what was promised.

37 For yet in a very little while,
the Coming One will come and not delay.
38 But my righteous one will live by faith;
and if he draws back,
I have no pleasure in him.

39 But we are not those who draw back and are destroyed, but those who have faith and are saved.

Day 5

Confidence in God

HABAKKUK · ZEPHANIAH · HAGGAI · NAHUM ·

HABAKKUK 3, PSALM 17, JOHN 1:14–18, GALATIANS 3:11

HABAKKUK 3

Habakkuk's Third Prayer

1 A prayer of the prophet Habakkuk. According to *Shigionoth*.

2 LORD, I have heard the report about you;
LORD, I stand in awe of your deeds.
Revive your work in these years;
make it known in these years.
In your wrath remember mercy!

3 God comes from **Teman**,
the Holy One from **Mount Paran**. *Selah*
His splendor covers the heavens,
and the earth is full of his praise.
4 His brilliance is like light;
rays are flashing from his hand.
This is where his power is hidden.
5 Plague goes before him,
and pestilence follows in his steps.
6 He stands and shakes the earth;
he looks and startles the nations.
The age-old mountains break apart;
the ancient hills sink down.
His pathways are ancient.
7 I see the tents of **Cushan** in distress;
the tent curtains of the land of **Midian** tremble.
8 Are you angry at the rivers, LORD?
Is your wrath against the rivers?
Or is your rage against the sea

when you ride on your horses,
your victorious chariot?
9 You took the sheath from your bow;
the arrows are ready to be used with an oath. *Selah*
You split the earth with rivers.
10 The mountains see you and shudder;
a downpour of water sweeps by.
The deep roars with its voice
and lifts its waves high.
11 Sun and moon stand still in their lofty residence,
at the flash of your flying arrows,
at the brightness of your shining spear.
12 You march across the earth with indignation;
you trample down the nations in wrath.
13 You come out to save your people,
to save your anointed.
You crush the leader of the house of the wicked
and strip him from foot to neck. *Selah*
14 You pierce his head
with his own spears;
his warriors storm out to scatter us,
gloating as if ready to secretly devour the weak.
15 You tread the sea with your horses,
stirring up the vast water.

Habakkuk's Confidence in God Expressed

16 I heard, and I trembled within;
my lips quivered at the sound.
Rottenness entered my bones;
I trembled where I stood.
Now I must quietly wait for the day of distress
to come against the people invading us.
17 Though the fig tree does not bud
and there is no fruit on the vines,
though the olive crop fails
and the fields produce no food,
though the flocks disappear from the pen
and there are no herds in the stalls,

NOTES

NOTES

18 yet I will celebrate in the LORD;
I will rejoice in the God of my salvation!
19 The LORD my Lord is my strength;
he makes my feet like those of a deer
and enables me to walk on mountain heights!

For the choir director: on stringed instruments.

PSALM 17

A Prayer for Protection

A prayer of David.

1 LORD, hear a just cause;
pay attention to my cry;
listen to my prayer—
from lips free of deceit.
2 Let my vindication come from you,
for you see what is right.
3 You have tested my heart;
you have examined me at night.
You have tried me and found nothing evil;
I have determined that my mouth will not sin.
4 Concerning what people do:
by the words from your lips
I have avoided the ways of the violent.
5 My steps are on your paths;
my feet have not slipped.

6 I call on you, God,
because you will answer me;
listen closely to me; hear what I say.
7 Display the wonders of your faithful love,
Savior of all who seek refuge
from those who rebel against your right hand.
8 Protect me as the pupil of your eye;
hide me in the shadow of your wings
9 from the wicked who treat me violently,
my deadly enemies who surround me.

[10] They are uncaring;
their mouths speak arrogantly.
[11] They advance against me; now they surround me.
They are determined
to throw me to the ground.
[12] They are like a lion eager to tear,
like a young lion lurking in ambush.

[13] Rise up, LORD!
Confront him; bring him down.
With your sword, save me from the wicked.
[14] With your hand, LORD, save me from men,
from men of the world
whose portion is in this life:
You fill their bellies with what you have in store;
their sons are satisfied,
and they leave their surplus to their children.

[15] But I will see your face in righteousness;
when I awake, I will be satisfied with your presence.

Dig Deeper

-

Observe
What is happening in the text?

Reflect
What does it teach me about God?

Apply
What is my response?

JOHN 1:14–18

[14] The Word became flesh and dwelt among us. We observed his glory,
the glory as the one and only Son from the Father, full of grace and truth.
[15] (John testified concerning him and exclaimed, "This was the one of
whom I said, 'The one coming after me ranks ahead of me, because he
existed before me.'") [16] Indeed, we have all received grace upon grace from
his fullness, [17] for the law was given through Moses; grace and truth came
through Jesus Christ. [18] No one has ever seen God. The one and only Son,
who is himself God and is at the Father's side—he has revealed him.

GALATIANS 3:11

Now it is clear that no one is justified before God by the law, because the righteous will live by faith.

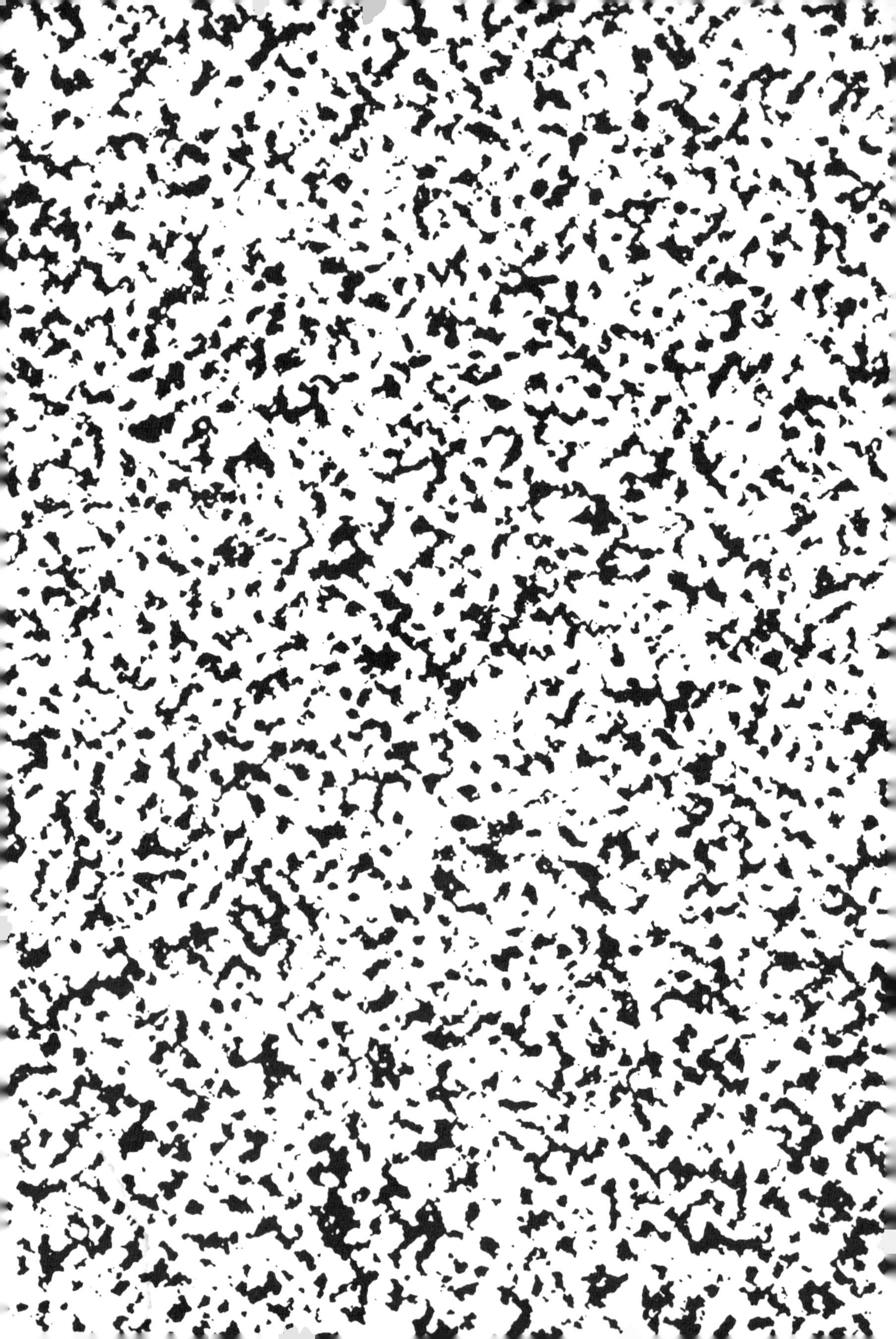

GIVE THANKS FOR THE BOOK OF

Habakkuk

The book of Habakkuk addresses the common struggle to understand God's actions in the world while calling us to faith in God's good purposes. Habakkuk's message that the righteous will live by faith prepared the way for the greater understanding of this truth in the New Testament, which emphasizes salvation through faith in Christ (Rm 1:17; Gl 3:11; Heb 10:38–39).

f
e
d

DAY 6

Grace Day

-

Use today to pray, rest, and reflect on this week's reading, giving thanks for the grace that is ours in Christ.

Yet I will celebrate in the LORD; I will rejoice in the God of my salvation! The LORD my Lord is my strength; he makes my feet like those of a deer and enables me to walk on mountain heights!

Habakkuk 3:18–19

DATE

/ /

DAY 7

Weekly Truth

-

Scripture is God-breathed and true. When we memorize it, we carry the gospel with us wherever we go.

This week we will memorize the key verse for Nahum.

DATE / /

The LORD is good, a stronghold in a day of distress; he cares for those who take refuge in him.

Nahum 1:7

The Minor Prophets

Timeline

760 BC

Jonah travels to Nineveh

735 BC

Damascus and Israel attack Jerusalem and Judah

722 BC

Israel falls to Assyria, leaving only the southern kingdom

Israelites from the ten northern tribes are taken into exile

715-686 BC

King Hezekiah of Judah

750

701 BC

King Sennacherib of Assyria captures and devastates Judah

700 BC

Nineveh established as the capital of the Assyrian Empire

689 BC

King Sennacherib of Assyria destroys the city of Babylon

686-642 BC

King Manasseh of Judah

675 BC

Start of Nahum's ministry

665 BC

Assyria destroys Thebes, the capital of Egypt

642-640 BC

King Amon of Judah

700

650

640–609 BC
King Josiah of Judah

631 BC
King Josiah's initial reforms

630 BC
Nahum's prophecy against Nineveh

626 BC
Zephaniah's prophetic call

621 BC
Book of the Law found and read publicly, continuing Josiah's reforms

612 BC
Fall of Nineveh

End of Zephaniah's ministry

ca 610 BC
Start of Habakkuk's ministry

609 BC
Pharaoh Neco invades Judah

Fall of Assyria

609–599 BC
King Jehoiakim of Judah

605 BC
First Babylonian siege of Judah

598 BC
King Jehoiachin of Judah comes to power

597 BC
End of Habakkuk's prophetic ministry

Second Babylonian invasion

People of Judah taken into exile

588 BC
King Nebuchadnezzar of Babylon takes Jerusalem

586 BC
Temple and wall of Jerusalem destroyed

586–538 BC
Babylonian Exile

600

520 BC

Haggai's ministry

538 BC

Decree of Cyrus allows exiles to return to Judah to rebuild the temple

536 BC

Foundation of new temple laid

515 BC

Decree of Darius allows rebuilding of the temple in Jerusalem to continue

Temple construction complete

550

KEY VERSE

The Lord your God is among you, a warrior who saves. He will rejoice over you with gladness. He will be quiet in his love. He will delight in you with singing.

Zephaniah 3:17

ON THE TIMELINE

Evidence in the text indicates the book of Zephaniah was written sometime between 640 and 612 BC. Zephaniah 1:1 refers to King Josiah's reign (around 640–609 BC), and 2:13–15 prophesies Nineveh's fall, which occurred in 612 BC. This message was given to Judah about a decade before the first deportation to Babylon in 605 BC.

A LITTLE BACKGROUND

King Josiah's father, King Amon (Zph 1:1), was a wicked man, as was his father King Manasseh before him (2Kg 21:1–7, 11, 16, 20–22). This heritage of wickedness helps explain the rampant idolatry in the land when Josiah inherited the throne in 640 BC. While the new king struggled to squelch idolatry in Judah (Zph 1:4-9), pagan and "orthodox" priests led worship of the Lord while also bowing before Baal, Molech, and other pagan gods (Zph 1:4–6). The public reading of the book of the Law (ca 621 BC) helped bring the people to repentance, prompting them to tear down the altars to their false gods (Zph 1:3-4; 2 Kg 23:1–14).

MESSAGE & PURPOSE

In view of the impending destruction of the "day of the LORD" (Zph 1:7–18; 2:2-3), Zephaniah's primary purpose was to extend an urgent invitation. He urged the people of Judah to seek the Lord alone in righteousness and humility (Zph 2:1-3). The immediate purpose was to warn idolatrous Judah of the Lord's imminent judgment (Zph 1:4–13), but the ultimate purpose was to call out a "remnant" from all nations (Zph 2:7–9; 3:12–13; 3:9–10) to trust in the Lord.

Day 8

The Great Day of the Lord

ZEPHANIAH 1, ROMANS 9:19–24, 2 PETER 3:8–10

ZEPHANIAH 1

1 The word of the LORD that came to Zephaniah son of Cushi, son of Gedaliah, son of Amariah, son of Hezekiah, in the days of **Josiah** son of **Amon**, king of Judah.

The Great Day of the LORD

2 I will completely sweep away everything
from the face of the earth—
this is the LORD's declaration.
3 I will sweep away people and animals;
I will sweep away the birds of the sky
and the fish of the sea,
and the ruins along with the wicked.
I will cut off mankind
from the face of the earth.
This is the LORD's declaration.

4 I will stretch out my hand against Judah
and against all the residents of Jerusalem.
I will cut off every vestige of **Baal**
from this place,
the names of the pagan priests
along with the priests;
5 those who bow in worship on the rooftops
to the stars in the sky;
those who bow and pledge loyalty to the Lord
but also pledge loyalty to **Milcom**;
6 and those who turn back from following the LORD,
who do not seek the LORD or inquire of him.

7 Be silent in the presence of the Lord God,
for the day of the Lord is near.
Indeed, the Lord has prepared a sacrifice;
he has consecrated his guests.

8 On the day of the Lord's sacrifice
I will punish the officials, the king's sons,
and all who are dressed in foreign clothing.
9 On that day I will punish
all who skip over the threshold,
who fill their master's house
with violence and deceit.

10 On that day—
this is the Lord's declaration—
there will be an outcry from the **Fish Gate**,
a wailing from the **Second District**,
and a loud crashing from the hills.
11 Wail, you residents of **the Hollow**,
for all the merchants will be silenced;
all those loaded with silver will be cut off.

12 And at that time I will search Jerusalem with lamps
and punish those who settle down comfortably,
who say to themselves:
The Lord will not do good or evil.
13 Their wealth will become plunder
and their houses a ruin.
They will build houses but never live in them,
plant vineyards but never drink their wine.

NOTES

14 The great day of the LORD is near, near and rapidly approaching.

Listen, the day of the LORD—
then the warrior's cry is bitter.
15 That day is a day of wrath,
a day of trouble and distress,
a day of destruction and desolation,
a day of darkness and gloom,
a day of clouds and total darkness,
16 a day of trumpet blast and battle cry
against the fortified cities,
and against the high corner towers.
17 I will bring distress on mankind,
and they will walk like the blind
because they have sinned against the LORD.
Their blood will be poured out like dust
and their flesh like dung.
18 Their silver and their gold
will be unable to rescue them
on the day of the LORD's wrath.
The whole earth will be consumed
by the fire of his jealousy,
for he will make a complete,
yes, a horrifying end
of all the inhabitants of the earth.

ROMANS 9:19–24

19 You will say to me, therefore, "Why then does he still find fault?
For who can resist his will?" 20 But who are you, a mere man, to talk
back to God? Will what is formed say to the one who formed it, "Why
did you make me like this?" 21 Or has the potter no right over the clay,
to make from the same lump one piece of pottery for honor and another
for dishonor? 22 And what if God, wanting to display his wrath and

to make his power known, endured with much patience objects of wrath prepared for destruction? 23 And what if he did this to make known the riches of his glory on objects of mercy that he prepared beforehand for glory— 24 on us, the ones he also called, not only from the Jews but also from the Gentiles?

2 PETER 3:8–10

8 Dear friends, don't overlook this one fact: With the Lord one day is like
a thousand years, and a thousand years like one day. 9 The Lord does not
delay his promise, as some understand delay, but is patient with you, not wanting any to perish but all to come to repentance.

10 But the day of the Lord will come like a thief; on that day the heavens will pass away with a loud noise, the elements will burn and be dissolved, and the earth and the works on it will be disclosed.

Dig Deeper

-

Observe
What is happening in the text?

Reflect
What does it teach me about God?

Apply
What is my response?

Day 9

A Call to Repentance

ZEPHANIAH 2

PSALM 27:7-10

ROMANS 11:1-6

A Call to Repentance

1 Gather yourselves together;
gather together, undesirable nation,
2 before the decree takes effect
and the day passes like chaff,
before the burning of the LORD's anger overtakes you,
before the day of the LORD's anger overtakes you.
3 Seek the LORD, all you humble of the earth,
who carry out what he commands.
Seek righteousness, seek humility;
perhaps you will be concealed
on the day of the LORD's anger.

Judgment Against the Nations

4 For **Gaza** will be abandoned,
and **Ashkelon** will become a ruin.
Ashdod will be driven out at noon,
and **Ekron** will be uprooted.
5 Woe, inhabitants of the seacoast,
nation of the **Cherethites**!
The word of the LORD is against you,
Canaan, land of the **Philistines**:
I will destroy you until there is no one left.
6 The seacoast will become pasturelands
with caves for shepherds and pens for sheep.
7 The coastland will belong
to the remnant of the house of Judah;
they will find pasture there.
They will lie down in the evening
among the houses of Ashkelon,
for the LORD their God will return to them
and restore their fortunes.

8 I have heard the taunting of **Moab**
and the insults of the **Ammonites**,
who have taunted my people
and threatened their territory.

NOTES

9 Therefore, as I live—
this is the declaration of the LORD of Armies, the God of Israel—
Moab will be like **Sodom**
and the Ammonites like **Gomorrah**:
a place overgrown with weeds,
a salt pit, and a perpetual wasteland.
The remnant of my people will plunder them;
the remainder of my nation will dispossess them.
10 This is what they get for their pride,
because they have taunted and acted arrogantly
against the people of the LORD of Armies.
11 The LORD will be terrifying to them
when he starves all the gods of the earth.
Then all the distant coasts and islands of the nations
will bow in worship to him,
each in its own place.

12 You Cushites will also be slain by my sword.

13 He will also stretch out his hand against the north
and destroy Assyria;
he will make Nineveh a desolate ruin,
dry as the desert.
14 Herds will lie down in the middle of it,
every kind of wild animal.
Both eagle owls and herons
will roost in the capitals of its pillars.
Their calls will sound from the window,
but devastation will be on the threshold,
for he will expose the cedar work.
15 This is the jubilant city
that lives in security,
that thinks to herself:
I exist, and there is no one else.
What a desolation she has become,
a place for wild animals to lie down!
Everyone who passes by her
scoffs and shakes his fist.

PSALM 27:7–10

7 LORD, hear my voice when I call;
be gracious to me and answer me.
8 My heart says this about you:
"Seek his face."
LORD, I will seek your face.
9 Do not hide your face from me;
do not turn your servant away in anger.
You have been my helper;
do not leave me or abandon me,
God of my salvation.
10 Even if my father and mother abandon me,
the LORD cares for me.

Dig Deeper

-

Observe
What is happening in the text?

Reflect
What does it teach me about God?

Apply
What is my response?

ROMANS 11:1–6

Israel's Rejection Not Total

1 I ask, then, has God rejected his people? Absolutely not! For I too am
an Israelite, a descendant of Abraham, from the tribe of Benjamin. 2 God
has not rejected his people whom he foreknew. Or don't you know what the Scripture says in the passage about Elijah—how he pleads with God
against Israel? 3 Lord, they have killed your prophets and torn down your
altars. I am the only one left, and they are trying to take my life! 4 But
what was God's answer to him? I have left seven thousand for myself who
have not bowed down to Baal. 5 In the same way, then, there is also at the
present time a remnant chosen by grace. 6 Now if by grace, then it is not
by works; otherwise grace ceases to be grace.

Day 10

Woe to Oppressive Jerusalem

ZEPHANIAH 3, ISAIAH 30:18, HEBREWS 7:22–28

ZEPHANIAH 3

Woe to Oppressive Jerusalem

1 Woe to the city that is rebellious and defiled,
the oppressive city!
2 She has not obeyed;
she has not accepted discipline.
She has not trusted in the LORD;
she has not drawn near to her God.
3 The princes within her are roaring lions;
her judges are wolves of the night,
which leave nothing for the morning.
4 Her prophets are reckless—
treacherous men.
Her priests profane the sanctuary;
they do violence to instruction.
5 The righteous LORD is in her;
he does no wrong.
He applies his justice morning by morning;
he does not fail at dawn,
yet the one who does wrong knows no shame.

6 I have cut off nations;
their corner towers are destroyed.
I have laid waste their streets,
with no one to pass through.
Their cities lie devastated,
without a person, without an inhabitant.
7 I thought: You will certainly fear me

and accept correction.
Then her dwelling place
would not be cut off
based on all that I had allocated to her.
However, they became more corrupt
in all their actions.
8 Therefore, wait for me—
this is the LORD's declaration—
until the day I rise up for plunder.
For my decision is to gather nations,
to assemble kingdoms,
in order to pour out my indignation on them,
all my burning anger;
for the whole earth will be consumed
by the fire of my jealousy.

Final Restoration Promised

9 For I will then restore
pure speech to the peoples
so that all of them may call
on the name of the LORD
and serve him with a single purpose.
10 From beyond the **rivers of Cush**
my supplicants, my dispersed people,
will bring an offering to me.
11 On that day you will not be put to shame
because of everything you have done
in rebelling against me.

NOTES

For then I will remove
from among you your jubilant, arrogant people,
and you will never again be haughty
on my holy mountain.
12 I will leave
a meek and humble people among you,
and they will take refuge in the name of the LORD.
13 The remnant of Israel will no longer
do wrong or tell lies;
a deceitful tongue will not be found
in their mouths.
They will pasture and lie down,
with nothing to make them afraid.

14 Sing for joy, Daughter **Zion**;
shout loudly, Israel!
Be glad and celebrate with all your heart,
Daughter Jerusalem!
15 The LORD has removed your punishment;
he has turned back your enemy.
The **King of Israel**, the LORD, is among you;
you need no longer fear harm.
16 On that day it will be said to Jerusalem:
"Do not fear;
Zion, do not let your hands grow weak.
17 The LORD your God is among you,
a warrior who saves.
He will rejoice over you with gladness.
He will be quiet in his love.
He will delight in you with singing."

18 I will gather those who have been driven
from the appointed festivals;
they will be a tribute from you
and a reproach on her.
19 Yes, at that time
I will deal with all who oppress you.
I will save the lame and gather the outcasts;

I will make those who were disgraced
throughout the earth
receive praise and fame.
20 At that time I will bring you back,
yes, at the time I will gather you.
I will give you fame and praise
among all the peoples of the earth,
when I restore your fortunes before your eyes.
The LORD has spoken.

Dig Deeper

-

Observe
What is happening in the text?

Reflect
What does it teach me about God?

Apply
What is my response?

ISAIAH 30:18

The LORD's Mercy to Israel
Therefore the LORD is waiting to show you mercy,
and is rising up to show you compassion,
for the LORD is a just God.
All who wait patiently for him are happy.

HEBREWS 7:22–28

22 Because of this oath, Jesus has also become the guarantee of a better covenant.

23 Now many have become Levitical priests, since they are prevented
by death from remaining in office. 24 But because he remains forever,
he holds his priesthood permanently. 25 Therefore, he is able to save
completely those who come to God through him, since he always lives
to intercede for them.

26 For this is the kind of high priest we need: holy, innocent, undefiled,
separated from sinners, and exalted above the heavens. 27 He doesn't need
to offer sacrifices every day, as high priests do—first for their own sins,
then for those of the people. He did this once for all time when he offered
himself. 28 For the law appoints as high priests men who are weak, but
the promise of the oath, which came after the law, appoints a Son, who
has been perfected forever.

GIVE THANKS FOR THE BOOK OF

Zephaniah

The promise of a remnant illustrates God's amazing grace alongside His just wrath toward the wicked (Nah 1:2–8). God would judge the proud (Zph 2:8–11, 13–15; 3:11) and preserve the humble, and Zephaniah invited everyone who humbly obeyed the Lord to seek Him for deliverance (2:2–3). The New Testament highlights the beautiful truth that all people are invited to be part of what Paul calls a "remnant chosen by grace" (Rm 11:5)—those who receive eternal salvation through faith in Christ.

HABAKKUK · ZEPHANIAH · HAGGAI · NAHUM

KEY VERSE

"The final glory of this house will be greater than the first," says the LORD of Armies. "I will provide peace in this place"—this is the declaration of the LORD of Armies.

Haggai 2:9

ON THE TIMELINE

Haggai is written to the people in postexilic Jerusalem, about 520 BC. The temple had been destroyed in 586 BC during Nebuchadnezzar's final siege of Jerusalem, and Haggai's message encouraged the returned people to continue the rebuilding of the temple. There is no statement specifically identifying who wrote this book, but the words recorded are repeatedly connected to what God spoke to the prophet Haggai (1:1, 3, 13; 2:1, 10, 14, 20).

A LITTLE BACKGROUND

After the Persian king Cyrus defeated Babylon, he issued a decree in 538 BC that allowed the exiled nations in Babylon to return to their homelands (Ezr 1:1–4). Because of this, Sheshbazzar (Ezr 1:8–11) led about 43,000 Jewish pilgrims back to Judah to rebuild the temple in Jerusalem (Ezr 2:64–65). After the Samaritan people frustrated the rebuilding efforts and a new governor of the region refused to approve the construction, the Jewish people began to lose hope. However, in 515 BC, Darius (now king of Persia) issued a decree that allowed the Jewish people to continue rebuilding the temple.

MESSAGE & PURPOSE

Haggai challenged the discouraged people in Jerusalem to examine the way they were living. He called them to set new priorities that would please God, glorifying Him in their rebuilding of the temple. Haggai argued that the people should not focus on their own needs (Hg 1:4), become discouraged because the temple was not as glorious as Solomon's (Hg 2:3), be unclean and unholy (Hg 2:10–14), or feel useless and powerless (Hg 2:20–23). The restoration of the temple was a sign that God had not revoked His covenant. It showed He was with the remnant and His promises were indeed being fulfilled.

Day 11

Command to Rebuild the Temple

HAGGAI 1

EZRA 4:24

EZRA 5:1-5

EPHESIANS 2:19-22

HABAKKUK · ZEPHANIAH · HAGGAI · NAHUM

Command to Rebuild the Temple

1 In the second year of **King Darius**, on the first day of the sixth month,
the word of the LORD came through the prophet Haggai to **Zerubbabel**
son of Shealtiel, the governor of Judah, and to **Joshua son of Jehozadak**,
the high priest:

2 "The LORD of Armies says this: These people say: The time has not come
for the house of the LORD to be rebuilt."

3 The word of the LORD came through the prophet Haggai: 4 "Is it a time
for you yourselves to live in your paneled houses, while this house lies
in ruins?" 5 Now, the LORD of Armies says this: "Think carefully about
your ways:

> 6 You have planted much
> but harvested little.
> You eat
> but never have enough to be satisfied.
> You drink
> but never have enough to be happy.
> You put on clothes
> but never have enough to get warm.
> The wage earner puts his wages
> into a bag with a hole in it."

7 The LORD of Armies says this: "Think carefully about your ways. 8 Go
up into the hills, bring down lumber, and build the house; and I will be
pleased with it and be glorified," says the LORD. 9 "You expected much,
but then it amounted to little. When you brought the harvest to your
house, I ruined it. Why?" This is the declaration of the LORD of Armies.
"Because my house still lies in ruins, while each of you is busy with his
own house.

> 10 So on your account,
> the skies have withheld the dew
> and the land its crops.

NOTES

[11] I have summoned a drought
on the fields and the hills,
on the grain, new wine, fresh oil,
and whatever the ground yields,
on man and animal,
and on all that your hands produce."

The People's Response

[12] Then Zerubbabel son of Shealtiel, the high priest Joshua son of Jehozadak, and the entire remnant of the people obeyed the LORD their God and the words of the prophet Haggai, because the LORD their God had sent him. So the people feared the LORD.

[13] Then Haggai, the LORD's messenger, delivered the LORD's message to the people:

"I am with you—this is the LORD's declaration."

[14] The LORD roused the spirit of Zerubbabel son of Shealtiel, governor of Judah, the spirit of the high priest Joshua son of Jehozadak, and the spirit of all the remnant of the people. They began work on the house of the LORD of Armies, their God, [15] on the twenty-fourth day of the sixth month, in the second year of King Darius.

EZRA 4:24

Rebuilding of the Temple Resumed

Now the construction of God's house in Jerusalem had stopped and remained at a standstill until the second year of the reign of King Darius of Persia.

EZRA 5:1-5

[1] But when the prophets Haggai and Zechariah son of Iddo prophesied to the Jews who were in Judah and Jerusalem, in the name of the God of Israel who was over them, [2] Zerubbabel son of Shealtiel and Jeshua son of

Jozadak began to rebuild God's house in Jerusalem. The prophets of God were with them, helping them.

[3] At that time Tattenai the governor of the region west of the Euphrates River, Shethar-bozenai, and their colleagues came to the Jews and asked, "Who gave you the order to rebuild this temple and finish this structure?" [4] They also asked them, "What are the names of the workers who are constructing this building?" [5] But God was watching over the Jewish elders. These men wouldn't stop them until a report was sent to Darius, so that they could receive written instructions about this matter.

Dig Deeper

-

Observe
What is happening in the text?

Reflect
What does it teach me about God?

Apply
What is my response?

EPHESIANS 2:19–22

[19] So then you are no longer foreigners and strangers, but fellow citizens with the saints, and members of God's household, [20] built on the foundation of the apostles and prophets, with Christ Jesus himself as the cornerstone. [21] In him the whole building, being put together, grows into a holy temple in the Lord. [22] In him you are also being built together for God's dwelling in the Spirit.

Day 12

Encouragement and Promise

HAGGAI 2

ROMANS 8:9–10

HEBREWS 12:26

HAGGAI 2

NOTES

Encouragement and Promise

1 On the twenty-first day of the seventh month, the word of the Lord
came through the prophet Haggai: 2 "Speak to Zerubbabel son of
Shealtiel, governor of Judah, to the high priest Joshua son of Jehozadak,
and to the remnant of the people: 3 'Who is left among you who saw this
house in its former glory? How does it look to you now? Doesn't it seem
to you like nothing by comparison? 4 Even so, be strong, Zerubbabel—
this is the Lord's declaration. Be strong, Joshua son of Jehozadak,
high priest. Be strong, all you people of the land—this is the Lord's
declaration. Work! For I am with you—the declaration of the Lord of
Armies. 5 This is the promise I made to you when you came out of Egypt,
and my Spirit is present among you; don't be afraid.'"

6 For the Lord of Armies says this: "Once more, in a little while, I am
going to shake the heavens and the earth, the sea and the dry land. 7 I will
shake all the nations so that the treasures of all the nations will come, and
I will fill this house with glory," says the Lord of Armies. 8 "The silver
and gold belong to me"—this is the declaration of the Lord of Armies.

9 "The final glory of this house
will be greater than the first,"

says the Lord of Armies. "I will provide peace in this place"—this is the
declaration of the Lord of Armies.

From Deprivation to Blessing

10 On the twenty-fourth day of the ninth month, in the second year of
Darius, the word of the Lord came to the prophet Haggai: 11 "This is
what the Lord of Armies says: Ask the priests for a ruling. 12 If a man
is carrying consecrated meat in the fold of his garment, and it touches
bread, stew, wine, oil, or any other food, does it become holy?"

The priests answered, "No."

13 Then Haggai asked, "If someone defiled by contact with a corpse
touches any of these, does it become defiled?"

NOTES

The priests answered, "It becomes defiled."

14 Then Haggai replied, "So is this people, and so is this nation before
me—this is the LORD's declaration. And so is every work of their hands;
even what they offer there is defiled.

15 "Now from this day on, think carefully: Before one stone was placed
on another in the LORD's temple, 16 what state were you in? When
someone came to a grain heap of twenty measures, it only amounted
to ten; when one came to the winepress to dip fifty measures from the
vat, it only amounted to twenty. 17 I struck you—all the work of your
hands—with blight, mildew, and hail, but you didn't turn to me—this
is the LORD's declaration. 18 "From this day on, think carefully; from the
twenty-fourth day of the ninth month, from the day the foundation of
the LORD's temple was laid; think carefully. 19 Is there still seed left in the
granary? The vine, the fig, the pomegranate, and the olive tree have not
yet produced. But from this day on I will bless you."

Promise to Zerubbabel

20 The word of the LORD came to Haggai a second time on the twenty-
fourth day of the month: 21 "Speak to Zerubbabel, governor of Judah:
I am going to shake the heavens and the earth. 22 I will overturn royal
thrones and destroy the power of the Gentile kingdoms. I will overturn
chariots and their riders. Horses and their riders will fall, each by his
brother's sword. 23 On that day"—this is the declaration of the LORD of
Armies—"I will take you, Zerubbabel son of Shealtiel, my servant"—this
is the LORD's declaration—"and make you like my signet ring, for I have
chosen you." This is the declaration of the LORD of Armies.

ROMANS 8:9–10

9 You, however, are not in the flesh, but in the Spirit, if indeed the Spirit
of God lives in you. If anyone does not have the Spirit of Christ, he does
not belong to him. 10 Now if Christ is in you, the body is dead because of
sin, but the Spirit gives life because of righteousness.

HEBREWS 12:26

His voice shook the earth at that time, but now he has promised, Yet once more I will shake not only the earth but also the heavens.

Dig Deeper

-

Observe
What is happening in the text?

Reflect
What does it teach me about God?

Apply
What is my response?

GIVE THANKS FOR THE BOOK OF

Haggai

Haggai admonished the postexilic Jewish people living in Jerusalem to choose God over what they thought would make them comfortable or happy. Their response to this challenge would be reflected in their work on the temple. In the New Testament, Jesus echoed Haggai's message: "But seek first the kingdom of God and his righteousness, and all these things will be provided for you" (Mt 6:33).

DAY 13 *Grace Day*

-

Use today to pray, rest, and reflect on this week's reading, giving thanks for the grace that is ours in Christ.

"The final glory of this house will be greater than the first," says the LORD of Armies. "I will provide peace in this place"—this is the declaration of the LORD of Armies.

Haggai 2:9

DATE / /

DAY 14

Weekly Truth

-

Scripture is God-breathed and true. When we memorize it, we carry the gospel with us wherever we go.

This week we will memorize the key verse for Zephaniah.

DATE ____ / ____ / ____

The LORD your God is among you, a warrior who saves. He will rejoice over you with gladness. He will be quiet in his love. He will delight in you with singing.

Zephaniah 3:17

GLOSSARY

THIS GLOSSARY EXPLORES KEY PEOPLE AND PLACES REFERENCED IN THE BOOKS OF NAHUM, HABAKKUK, ZEPHANIAH, AND HAGGAI.

Key People and Places

AMMONITES
AMON
ASSYRIA
BAAL
BASHAN
CANAAN
CARMEL
CHALDEANS
CHERETHITES
CUSH
CUSHAN
EGYPT
ELKOSHITE
FISH GATE
GAZA, ASHKELON, ASHDOD, AND EKRON
HEZEKIAH
THE HOLLOW
ISRAEL
JERUSALEM
JOSHUA SON OF JEHOZADAK
JOSIAH
JUDAH
KING DARIUS
KING OF ASSYRIA
KING OF ISRAEL
LACHISH
LEBANON
LIBYA
LORD OF ARMIES
MIDIAN
MILCOM
MOAB
MOUNT PARAN
NILE
NINEVEH
PHILISTINES
PUT
RIVERS OF CUSH
SECOND DISTRICT
SENNACHERIB
SHEOL
SODOM AND GOMORRAH
TEMAN
THEBES
ZERUBBABEL SON OF SHEALTIEL
ZION

A-E

Ammonites PEOPLE
Ethnic group from the Ammon region, a territory northeast of the Dead Sea, who frequently opposed Israel. As descendants of Lot, they were considered kinsmen of the Moabites and the Israelites.

Amon PERSON
Idolatrous and evil king of Judah.

Assyria PLACE
An empire and civilization in northern Mesopotamia and a major opponent of Judah and Israel. Conquered the Northern Kingdom of Israel in 722 BC.

Baal DEITY
The Canaanite storm god often worshiped by Israel.

Bashan PLACE
A region northeast of the Jordan River known for its fertile land.

Canaan PLACE
The territory to the west of the Jordan River and the Dead Sea. The Canaanite people lived in the region of Canaan before the arrival of the Israelites and the Philistines and were descended from Noah's son Ham.

Carmel PLACE
A coastal mountain range in northern Israel known for its beauty and fertile land.

Chaldeans PEOPLE
An ethnic group in southern Babylonia; another name for the Babylonians.

Cherethites PEOPLE
A Philistine clan; another name for the Philistines.

Cush PLACE
Region in Africa south of Egypt; also called Ethiopia or Sheba.

Cushan PERSON
An Arab tribe living near Edom.

Egypt PLACE
One of the great civilizations of the ancient world, centered along the Nile in northeast Africa. God brought the Hebrew people out of slavery in Egypt to establish them as His people.

E-K

Elkoshite	PERSON	Someone from the region of Elkosh, which was likely in Judah.
Fish Gate	PLACE	The main northern city gate of Jerusalem.
Gaza, Ashkelon, Ashdod, and Ekron	PLACE	Four of five main Philistine cities located on the Mediterranean coast and coastal plain.
Hezekiah	PERSON	An ancestor of the prophet Zephaniah; the fourteenth king of Judah.
The Hollow	PLACE	The market district in Jerusalem.
Israel	PEOPLE	During the time of these Minor Prophets, inhabitants of Jerusalem were called Israel or Israelites since the northern tribes were in exile. Inhabitants of the southern kingdom of Judah were the only remaining descendants of the patriarch Jacob, who God renamed Israel.
Jerusalem	PLACE	Capital city of Judah.
Joshua son of Jehozadak	PERSON	First postexilic high priest. Carried the responsibility of guiding the people of Israel.
Josiah	PERSON	King of Judah (640-609 BC). Attempted religious reforms to bring Judah back to exclusive worship of God.
Judah	PEOPLE	One of the twelve tribes of Israel and the name of the southern kingdom during the divided monarchy.
King Darius	PERSON	Darius I (522-466 BC), the king of Persia. Issued a decree (ca 515 BC) allowing the Jewish people to finish building the second temple without interruption.
King of Assyria	PERSON	In Nahum, this likely refers to Ashurbanipal (ca 668-626 BC), the last great king of Assyria.

K-P

King of Israel	DEITY	The one true God.
Lachish	PLACE	An important city in Judah located southwest of Jerusalem.
Lebanon	PLACE	A mountainous region north of Israel noted for its forest.
Libya	PLACE	The desert nation of northern Africa west of the Nile valley of Egypt.
LORD of Armies	DEITY	A name for God that emphasizes His security, power, and strength in the face of His enemies as well as His authority as the leader of heavenly or earthly armies.
Midian	PLACE	A region southeast of Israel settled by the nomadic descendants of Midian, son of Abraham. Though initially friendly toward the Hebrew people, the Midianites, along with the Moabites, were often in conflict with the Israelites.
Milcom	DEITY	The god of the Ammonites.
Moab	PLACE	Region east of the Dead Sea. The Moabites, a tribe descended from Lot, became a frequent rival of Israel.
Mount Paran	PLACE	Likely the hilly region or upland wilderness forming the southern boundary of the promised land.
Nile	PLACE	A mighty river that surrounded Thebes and served as part of the defense system of the city.
Nineveh	PLACE	The capital of Assyria, the world superpower of the 600s BC.
Philistines	PEOPLE	Coastal people to the north and east of Israel; a persistent enemy of the Israelites.
Put	PLACE	A nation of uncertain location likely located along the north African coastline west of Libya and Egypt.

Rivers of Cush	PLACE	The Blue Nile and the White Nile.
Second District	PLACE	A city section north of the temple in Jerusalem.
Sennacherib	PERSON	King of the Assyrian Empire during the time of King Hezekiah (705–681 BC).
Sheol	PLACE	The underworld; the place where departed spirits go.
Sodom and Gomorrah	PLACE	Two infamous cities near the Dead Sea that were completely destroyed by God for their sins.
Teman	PLACE	A city in southern Edom.
Thebes	PLACE	Major Egyptian city that was captured and destroyed by the Assyrians around 663 BC.
Zerubbabel son of Shealtiel	PERSON	The governor of Judah and heir to the Davidic throne; carried the responsibility of guiding the people as Judah had no Hebrew king while under Persian control.
Zion	PLACE	An alternate name for Jerusalem, the city of David and home of the temple.

BIBLIOGRAPHY

Duvall, J. Scott. *The Story Begins: The Authority of the Bible, the Triune God, the Great and Good God.* Grand Rapids, MI: Kregel Publications, 2009.

Hays, J. Daniel. *The Message of the Prophets: A Survey of the Prophetic and Apocalyptic Books of the Old Testament.* Grand Rapids, MI: Zondervan, 2010.

FOR THE RECORD

Where did I study?

- ☐ HOME
- ☐ OFFICE
- ☐ CHURCH
- ☐ SCHOOL
- ☐ COFFEE SHOP
- ☐ OTHER:

WHAT WAS I LISTENING TO?

Song: ____________

Artist: ____________

Album: ____________

What time of day did I study?

- ☐ MORNING
- ☐ AFTERNOON
- ☐ NIGHT
- ☐ OTHER:

What was happening in the world?

What was happening in my life?

MY CLOSING PRAYER:

END DATE

____ / ____ / ____